NEW ALEXA M␣

Tutorial to Unlock The True Potential of Your Alexa Devices. The Complete User Guide with Instructions

by George Brown

New Alexa Manual

Introduction

———

This book contains proven steps and strategies on how to master Alexa enabled devices. If you have already bought an Amazon Echo and now wondering how to convert this device into your personal assistant, then this Alexa guide is for you. You can use several different Amazon devices to access Alexa. They are Amazon Echo, Echo Dot, Echo Show, Echo Spot, Echo Plus, and Sonos One and Fire TV interface for media. With so many different features and functions, first-time Alexa users can find it overwhelming to navigate them. This book will take you from the beginner to an Echo expert within a few hours. The guide contains specific step-by-step instructions that are well organized and easy to read. You will set up your Alexa enabled devices and start using all your smart devices and applications effortlessly.

CHAPTER ONE

Your Personal Assistant

Amazon introduced hands-free technology into the home of the general consumer when it launched its Echo device and the corresponding Alexa voice control system in 2014. Today, Alexa has become the most popular voice-activation software. In 2017 holiday season, Amazon Alexa device sales broke records. On Christmas day sale, Amazon's Alexa app occupied the number 1 slot on both the iPhone App Stores and Google Play stores free app charts.

Alexa uses a smart artificial intelligence program to teach from the commands it's given by the user. This makes it better and more user-friendly than other devices. With the skills API that lets anyone create their own commands for Alexa, this technology represents a drastic shift in how we as humans interact with machines.

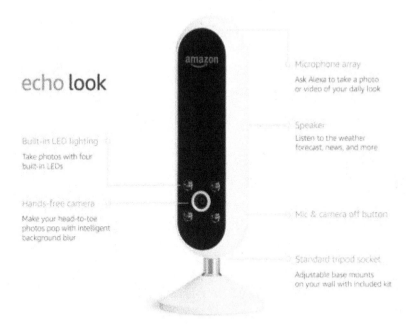

In 2017, Amazon released two new Alexa-enabled devices to their product line; the Echo Show and the Echo Look. Previous Echos only used listening devices such as speakers and microphones, but these newly introduced products have cameras, meaning Alexa can now see and hear you.

All of the Alexa-enabled devices are linked to an app that you can either view online (alexa.amazon.com) or download on your phone. In here, you can view the record of all your Alexa commands and you can customize the settings of the device. Amazon Fire tablets work best with Alexa, but it can be accessed on any device. If you are a first time Alexa user then go to Echosim.io - to scope it out with a device. Here you can taste Alexa capabilities and know if the app is the right choice for you. An Echo Dot cost only $30, so, it is not a big investment. The book is designed to introduce you all the ways Alexa can help you to manage your schedule and organize your life. Alexa is a perfect personal assistant for many users. She is always ready to answer your questions and complete your commands.

New additions – the Look and Show option of the Echo line makes Alexa even more useful. You can use the device as a personal stylist by using the camera on the look and plan your wardrobe, organize your closet and choose the clothes that suit you best.

Amazon has added a new feature to Alexa, known as Alexa Calling. The feature is similar to Skype or FaceTime application. This option gives you hands-free calling to another Alexa user and other facilities. Whether you are a new user, just bought a new device or used Alexa before, this book will show you everything you need to know about Alexa's capabilities as a personal assistant.

The Alexa voice control is extremely similar to using Siri on a smartphone. If you haven't used it before, do not worry because it is very easy to learn the basics. With more users, you and the device will get acquainted with each other and the device will become more helpful.

Amazon Echo – a wireless cylindrical speaker that can also function as a smart home hub was the first device that introduced Alexa in 2014. Since then Amazon has added several new devices that use Alexa. The Echo Tap portable version of the speaker while the Amazon Echo Dot is smaller, Echo designed for home use. Amazon's all FireTV products offer limited Alexa functionality. The price for the devices ranges from $30 for the Dot to $180 for the full-sized Echo.

All the previous Alexa build-in devices used speaker and microphone only. In 2017, Amazon included video to Alexa. In addition to audio performance as the Echo, the Echo Look includes a camera. With a 7" display and a front-facing camera, the Echo Show takes it one step further. Now you can use pictures and videos with Alexa. However, these devices are costlier (around $200 and $250), but they are still affordable, considering theirs functionalities.

The Alexa enabled devices are extremely easy to set-up and operate. The device will walk you through the set-up process when you take it out of the box and turn it on. Then you install the companion app on your smartphone and ready to use the device. This app is completely free and works on both Android and iOS devices. You can change any of the settings of your device and also see the command history or link your Alexa account to other services you would like to use it for.

The app will show you a list of devices that can use Alexa. When changing settings remember, some changes will affect all your devices, while others will apply to one type of devices. Spend some time exploring the setting menu to get a better idea of your device's functions and features.

When working on a smaller apartment, Alexa can hear and answer you. Amazon offers a Voice Remote for larger spaces that cost $30. Using the settings, you can pair any device with this Voice Remote.

Voice Recognition

As a smart assistant, Alexa can hear and process your commands as soon as you set it up. With more use, the device learns your voice. However, it might be wise to go through the voice training program when setting up a new device so there are no misunderstandings at the beginning. To locate the voice training app, go to the Menu, then choose settings. It can be a bit time consuming and can take about 30 minutes. When prompted, say around 25 phrases out loud. This will help Alexa to work with your speech and accent patterns more easily in the future.

Giving Commands

When you use the wake word, Alexa knows that you are talking about it. By default, the program is Alexa, but you can choose other options and you can choose from settings option. After saying the wake word, ask Alexa your questions. There are a few commands that you are going to say constantly, like Alexa, help, Alexa, cancel or Alexa, stop. If you don't hear Alexa responses to a question, just say "Alexa, say it again?" The app will repeat the last thing she said as many times as you want.

Alexa is linked to your Amazon account, so it will know your zip code, but you may need to enter your street address manually from the settings.

If you have multiple versions, then there is the issue of a device's location within your home. By default, your device will be given a default name (such as Mark's FireStick or Jill's Echo). However, it can be confusing if you have multiples of the same product. You can change the name of the device from the settings.

Multiple Users

You don't need to set up multiple user accounts to allow multiple people to use an Echo. Anyone who comes into your house can give Alexa orders just saying her name. To access the media libraries for multiple residents, you want to establish them as members of your household. Go to your Amazon account page and from the link "Household Profiles", you can adjust any settings to add multiple members.

Keep your housemate present when you are changing settings so they can give the necessary information. You can remove any user from the same settings, but remember they will be unable to join household for six months. Adding someone to your household gives them added benefits. They can access Amazon account, place orders and enjoy your Prime benefits. So, add only people you trust.

Separate user accounts on an Echo are limited. You can't add items to to-do lists or calendars of household users. The main value is that it allows Audiobooks, music and other files to be accessed from the household account through any connected Alexa device.

If you have children or roommates, you may want to limit their ability to place orders on your Amazon account by creating a passcode for voice purchases. You can do this from the Voice Purchasing menu on Alexa app. Also, you can turn off voice purchasing and avoid this problem.

Alerts and Alarms

From the Sounds & Notifications menu of the settings, you can change your volume settings and sound that plays for an alarm. There is a variety of sound option available for you to choose from. You can toggle audio confirmation from the Sounds & Notifications menu. In the default setting, you will know Alexa has heard the wake word or received your command because the ring on the top of the speaker will light up. If you placed it in a spot where it is not easily seen, then having it chime when it hears you can make sure you know when Alexa is listening.

Music and other Audio

The Amazon Echo was released as a wireless speaker. However, Alexa is much more than a speaker. It is a great hands-free and voice-controlled option for listening to your favorite songs, podcasts, and audiobook. By default, the Amazon Prime music is the music player on Alexa. If you have an account with others, such as Pandora, Spotify or iHeart-Radio, you can link these to your Alexa account and use them as your default player, instead.

To change the default setting, from Menu go to Settings. From your account choose Music & Media. Scroll down to "Customize my music service performances" and select "Choose default music services". Here you can select others as your main music player. Currently, iTunes/ Apple Music and Google Play aren't compatible with Alexa. You can use your Alexa equipped speakers as a regular Bluetooth speaker. You can do this by putting the device in Bluetooth pairing mode. Say "Alexa, pair" and your Echo will pair with your device. When finished, say "Alexa, disconnect" and it will go to the previous setting.

Alexa also offers direct integration with TuneIn. TuneIn is a service that gives you access to a large podcast library and an array of live radio stations. Just by saying its name, you can bring up the latest episode of a podcast. The downside is it will only bring up the most recent episode easily with voice command. You have to say "Play the previous episode" to get the prior episodes, but you have to say it again and again to reach your desired episode. If you want to listen to a specific episode, then you have to select it manually. Alexa can read you Audiobooks, too. To do this, you have to link your Audible account directly to your account and then say, "Alexa, read the audiobook" and say the title of the book. Also, you can have Alexa read from your Kindle library. But remember, Alexa will read the Kindle books in her robotic voice.

CHAPTER TWO

Setting Up Your Alexa

The idea behind the Echo and Alexa is to make it user-friendly so even a novice can use them. If you've never used an Echo device before, you will be surprised how easy it is to use. You just have to plug in the device and it will start working. You need to download the free Alexa app to control the settings and features of your device. You can install it on any smartphone that uses the Fire operating system and iOS devices (version 9.o and hither) and Android devices (version 5.0 and higher).

You can use Alexa on any laptop or Tablet. The new Fire HD tablets have Alexa capability installed. For other devices, you can simply go to **https://alexa.amazon.com** from any web browser. It is compatible with most popular browsers, including Microsoft Internet Explorer 10 or higher, Safari, Firefox and Chrome. Plug in your Echo device and install the Alexa app, and your setup is almost complete.

Single Echo Placement

The microphones on all iterations of the Echo uses advanced technology and has a wide range. Even with a lot of background noise, you can count on the Echo to hear you and respond in a large room. The important thing is the placement of your Echo device. Chose a spot that is ideal for voice command.

For general use, a kitchen or living room is a great choice. If you are living in a single apartment, place the Echo in a central location. You can use Alexa through the app on your phone if you are outside of its listening area. Also, you need to consider the strength of your Wi-Fi connection. If your living space is large, then place your Echo close to your Wi-Fi router.

MULTIPLE ECHO DEVICE Placement

In most cases, only one Echo device is not enough to bring Alexa connectivity to your entire home. You can buy inexpensive options like Echo Dot and make it easy to place an Alexa compatible device in every room, which will give you a truly smart home. Ensuring all your devices have a reliable Wi-Fi connection can be tricky. For larger spaces, you may need to upgrade your wireless network or buy a Wi-Fi extender.

Which Echo devices to place where is also an important issue. Most people buy a pack of Echo Dots to outfit an entire home with Alexa. The Echo Look and Echo Spot are designed for use in the bedroom. They look as the closet aid and the spot as a bedside alarm clock. An Echo Show is especially helpful in the kitchen. You can use the Echo Spatial Perception or ESP if you are using multiple Echo devices in your home to determine which device should respond to your commands. This will eliminate the problem of multiple Echo's hearing you and responding.

The ESP system is excellent for telling you which of your devices is physically closest to you. The downside is, sometimes it can take Alexa a bit longer to respond.

Smart Device set-up

The set-up process for each device you add to your smart home system will be slightly different. You need to keep in mind a few general tips. Firstly, not every smart device will be able to connect with Alexa as soon as you set it up. Even if you have an Echo Plus with an included smart home hub, you will need to set up an account or enable an associated skill through the devices' brand before it can function fully.

In most cases, you can simply say, Alexa, discover new devices, after adding a new one to your home. The Echo will scan and then add all the devices found right in the Alexa app. If this process doesn't work, you have a few options. By going into the Alexa app and looking for the "Smart Home" section, you can manually enable associated skill. From Smart Home, go to "Smart Home Skills". If you don't see a skill for your device, you may instead need to look for the appropriate recipe on Yonomi or IFTTT instead.

Lastly, you want to re-mane your smart devices so they are easier to find. To do this, go to "Manage My Content & Devices" section of the app. It will change the name for Alexa, but you may still need to go into the device itself and re-name it to make it consistent with Bluetooth devices.

Choose a name that is easy to remember, unique and descriptive. If you would like to use multiple names to refer to the same device, you can set this up using groups.

CHAPTER THREE

Amazon Devices

A mazon Echo Look

You might be wondering what Echo look is and what its best features are. In this chapter, we are going to discuss detail tips and tricks for this new device.

Amazon Echo Look

Amazon Echo Look is an advancement on the original Echo system. If you need an assistant to pick you the perfect, then Echo Look can help you. First, you take a photo and the device will help you figure out recommendations. You can use this with the original Alexa features, such as a home cooking appliance, music, and news. You can use it for many different functions.

After purchasing, you open the box and find the items listed below:

The Amazon Echo Look Device

The Amazon Echo Look is Amazon's first device with a voice-activated camera. The Echo Look mimics the shape of an oversized pill – it is a cylinder with rounded ends. The device has the ability to sit on a top of a desk or it can be mounted with the wall mounting kit it includes. This kit includes instructions, anchors, screws, and wall plates. The device also includes:

- Quick start guide
- Power adapter with a 7.9-foot cable.
- Things to try card

The Amazon Echo Look can be directly compared to the Amazon Echo. Although they shaped differently, the two devices are quite similar.

Alexa as your stylist

With Amazon Echo Look, Alexa now becomes your stylist and her main goal is to make you look stunning. This device is intended to be near your closet or your bedroom. By simply using your voice, the Echo Look allows you to take full-length photos of your hourly, daily and weekly look. The camera allows you to blur the background, so your outfit becomes more noticeable. The Echo Look provides the ability for users to get outfit suggestions for a specific time frame, for immediate use or even the next day. You can plan your outfits in advance with this feature.

You can create a Look Book and share your outfits with the world. You can send feedback to the Style Check team at **support@stylechecked.com** and submit your opinion.

How it works

You only need to provide StyleCheck a location and a time to get started with your outfit submissions. StyleCheck will then recommend an outfit that goes with the weather. New features are constantly being added to make your fashion life easier. Here are the benefits of StyleCheck:

- Lowers your stress on dress choosing. Stay appropriately dressed for all occasions.
- Get outfit certainty. No more guessing and second-guessing.
- With Echo Look, you will always be prepared for the weather.

Style Check Features

- Receive outfit suggestions for a specific time frame, for instant use or even the next day so you can plan your outfit in advance.
- Fast and easy to use. You can get outfit recommendations within one minute.
- Receive outfit recommendations for any location.

For the nerds, here is how StyleCheck helps you:

- Outfit suggestions based on uses Perez-In either Solar Radiation models
- ASHRAE based thermal comfort model techniques
- Accurate Weather Data from **http://Forecast.io**
- Uses clothing thermal insulation or CLO ratings

The Echo Look needs a way to collect the visual information to be able to accurately judge visual information on your outfit. The Look camera collects light or an image, which has bounced off an object and records it using a sensor. Once this is finished, the information is then rendered in binary code. The binary code is the computer's language of choice. The imagery is then assessed and judged.

This process removes a lot of stress when it comes to dressing properly and also save you time. If you want to, you can simply skip the time frame when you have finished giving the location. With its Echo Look app, the echo look allows you to get a live view of your outfit. Alexa can even take a short video of you so you can see yourself from every angle.

The camera and the video functionality make it easier to get a full view of your outfit. The Echo Look's camera is enclosed by several small LED Lights. They aim to provide you a perfect, well-lit image. You can activate the camera by using Alexa's wake word and saying "take a photo". For example, when you say, Alexa, take my photo," get ready for a photo. For video, say "Alexa, take a video". After capture, your photo or video is uploaded to Amazon's cloud servers. Then they are sent to the connected smartphone application.

You can also take pictures of various objects, blur them out and only have the focus on the object. You can use various features to enable Alexa to find information. For example, you see a strange insect in your home. You take a photo. Then say "Alexa, ask Wikipedia what this insect is." Alexa can do this for you.

Same goes for your selfies. If you have Instagram or Facebook enabled, you can say "Alexa, upload this photo to Facebook with this caption…..". Then you can speak the captions. Alexa can do all these.

Removing Stains now

This is one of the popular features of Amazon Look; it can remove stains. If you get a stain and don't know how to remove it, then Echo Look can help you with it. The process is simple, take a photo of the stain, and ask "Alexa, ask Good housekeeping how to remove .... From ...." and you will get a complete set of steps on how to remove various stains from your clothing. You can do this with various garments and with upholstery or carpet. However, to use Alexa in this way, you need to make sure that you have Good housekeeping enabled on this. You can also use this skill with the Echo Show.

You can use this with the other Echo systems as well. You can also enable a security camera function on this if you want. If you are worried about voice listening and photo recording, then you can turn off watching and listening feature. Once these features are turned off, the device will illuminate a blue light and you need to use your wake word to turn on the features. Covering the camera is another way to make sure nothing is recorded.

CHAPTER FOUR

———

Safeguarding Your Privacy

ECHO LOOK

Many people are rightfully concerned about their video and face with the advent of the Echo Look. Essentially the Echo Look places a camera in your bedroom, but Amazon assures that all the data is safe. The security measures Amazon deploys include:

- Preventing third-party application installation on the Echo
- Rigorous security reviews

- Encryption of images and communication between the Echo Look, Echo Look app and the Amazon servers.
- Amazon doesn't provide any personal information to third parties or advertisers that display Amazon's interest-based ads.

Additionally, there is a mute button on the side of the device. You can use the button to mute the device and mask the camera. Also, you can unplug it when you don't need it. Your device remembers everything from the Amazon Alexa application and unplugging it will not cause any data loss.

Everything that can be done with Amazon Look selfies can already be done using the pictures that people have taken and posted online on a variety of social media sites. The major difference between selfies taken by you and Echo Look is that the device can give feedback on your style privately via the StyleCheck skill.

Taking pictures with a smartphone and then posting it on social media is significantly insecure. The Echo Look takes selfies to a new level, particularly for fashion and beauty bloggers who now have the power to give their readers 360 outfit views. They are able to get a hands-free, voice commanded, full frontal and 360 views.

CHAPTER FIVE

The Echo Show

In this chapter, we are going to discuss what Echo Show can do and its features.

Echo Show

Echo Show takes the Echo devices to the next level. This device will show you what you are looking for, and you can control everything easily with the sound of your voice. The system comes with a keyboard, a screen, and also some speakers to give you crisp sound that is perfect for indoor. It contains beam-forming technology and eight-microphone noise cancellation. Even when music is playing, the system will react based on your commands.

This feature enhances the Alexa system completely. You can use this to search information, call people and even read recipes. This device connects to Smart Home devices and you can control all of this with just your voice.

The device is about 7.4 inches high and 3.5 inches wide and weighs only about 41 ounces. The device has dual-band Wi-Fi support. It all connects with the simple AC power cord that comes in there. The cable is about 6 feet long. With Dolby stereo sound, the Echo Show is quite an impressive system.

Why would you need it?

If you love the Echo system, then this device is for you. Echo Show offers all the benefits of the previous plus gives you a screen. The system comes with a screen and you can connect to various sites to find recipes, look up information and get an accurate traffic and weather report.

The Echo Show helps connect your Smart Home devices in a much easier manner. You will be able to look at the various aspects of your devices with the screen and control them. You can call others with the system and it supports various music services. The device is for the people who are on the go.

Control everything with your voice

You can control everything with your voice command. You can ask Alexa to do virtually anything with this device. You can get messages and videos between all Echo devices with this device. You can talk to others about the Echo system or your app. The devices Drop in function allows you to check in on other rooms. For example, instead of using a baby monitor, you can ask Alexa to Drop In and check if everything is all right.

The Echo Show is a great system that will allow you to expand your reach with these devices to new heights. You can control your entire home with this system.

Setting up your Echo Show

Now we are going to discuss how to set up your Echo Show so you can use it in an efficient and rightful manner.

What Alexa can do

Alexa is a system that allows you to control your home and various devices with your voice. You can listen to music, watch movies, ask for weather and traffic update with this device. The Echo Show comes with a screen so you can play music, watch movies, look up information, and even find recipes with your voice.

Alexa is the system that will interact with you when it comes to the Echo Show. With Alexa, you can even control your home via Smart Home devices.

How to set up the Echo Show system?

Setting up the Alexa Echo Show system is easier than you think. You can set it up with only a few steps. First, you need to download the Alexa app, then sign in. You can get this from various web browsers and smartphones. This is available for the following systems: Android 5.0

or higher, iOS 9.0 or higher and FireOS 3.0 or higher. Depending on the mobile device you choose to use, you can download the Alexa app from either Google Play, Apple Store or Amazon AppStore. Check out **http://alexa.amazon.com** to check out the app.

Once it is all downloaded, you need to power up the Echo Show by simply plugging the device into any power outlet. Then follow the prompts to set it up, such as Wi-Fi connection, language, synchronizing your Amazon account, and reviewing the terms and conditions.

Next, you can then sync up your contacts and accounts and add all the fun stuff into there. You need to say the "wake word" if you want to sync up your voice to Alexa. The wake word is the word that will wake up the system. Whenever giving a command you have to start with saying "Alexa". Also, you can change the wake word.

Talking to Alexa

Talking to Alexa is pretty interactive, but you need to say a certain world first. You must say the wake word for the Echo Show and then your request. Also, if the Alexa name interferes with something, then you can change it to another. You can choose Computer, Echo, Amazon, and Alexa. To change the wake word, go to settings, choose the device go to wake word and from there you can select the world and then save.

If you want to change the wake word on the device directly instead of via the app, (your phone for example), go to settings, then device options, then wake word and then choose your word.

How to personalize your device

You can take a few steps to make the device really your device. For example, if you shift and your address needs to change, you can go to settings, choose your device, choose the device location and then edit. Change the address and choose to save. You can do this either on the Alexa app or on the device itself.

Alexa has a lot of skills and they can help you connect your home devices, check social media, play games, and even tell you about upcoming events. To activate skills, go to the app or say word Skills. From there you can choose a specific skill. When it is ready, open the page with the details and select the Enable Skill option. This is the same way you connect third-party movie and music services such as Netflix.

You can even have Alexa put calendar events in to find out what is next. Say "add ...... to my calendar for (day) at (time)" to add events to this. If you already know of an event, say "add the event to my calendar." You can delete any event manually or say "delete my (time) event" and it will be deleted.

You can add traffic information to your Echo Show to give you an idea of what your commute will be like. Go to settings, then accounts and choose traffic. From there put in the start and end point and choose to save changes to save the changes that you need to.

To get traffic updates, say "what's my commute?", "how is traffic, or what is traffic like right now?" The same goes for weather once you put in the device location and saying, "show me the weather", "what is the weather?" You can also ask if it will be hot or cold or it will rain or not. You can check the weather in various cities.

.

CHAPTER SIX

────

Other Amazon Devices

E cho Spot, Echo Second Generation, and Echo Plus

Amazon is introducing new devices every year. They vary in size and scope. This chapter will discuss on three new Echo devices: The Echo Spot, the Echo second generation and the Echo Plus.

All about the Echo Spot

The Echo Spot is the perfect device to put in your bedroom. The device has a small screen on it and acts as a smart alarm clock. The Echo Spot is an enhancement on Echo Show or Echo Dot. You can use it in other areas of your house. This is a great device if you need an Echo device with Bluetooth ability, music streaming, and video call making ability. The device is currently mainly focused on music and streaming it.

The Echo Plus and other Neat Features

In comparison to other Echo devices, the Echo Plus is essentially an enhanced microphone system. You can connect various gadgets to this device and it can work as a smart home device. The device has a 360-degree sound along with Dolby sound and a super enhanced microphone field. Echo Plus is able to recognize more devices when searched. You can connect to more smart home items.

It literally synchronizes everything by the cloud system and does the same with the apps and skills system that the other Echo devices had.

It will synchronize everything locally in a room. So for example, if you want to hook up some lights, you can let the Echo Plus synch it and it will hook it all up instantly.

This will make everything a smart home needs for you to work and live in. It also connects to Apple, Samsung and Nest devices, which gives you a wider range of what your echo device can hook up to.

2nd Generation Echo

| Charcoal Fabric | Heather Gray Fabric | Sandstone Fabric | Walnut Finish | Oak Finish | Silver Finish |

The Second Generation Echo and its Features

The second generation Echo is a lot cheaper than the first generation systems. With enhanced audio, it is a much simpler design. The device is half the price of the other one and it is much easier. It is smaller, a more customizable face and different from the first generation of models. The device does the same tasks as the other and can function using the wake word.

Choose the one that best fits you from these three models. If you are looking for a tinier device similar to the Echo Show, then the spot might be the one for you. You should consider the Echo Plus if you want to hook up a lot of smart home devices and don't want to have to manually put it all in. All of these devices do work with other Echo Systems, so keep them in mind.

You can get a battery-powered Echo tap, the second generation, a couple of Echo Dots and can set all of these all around the room. The Echo Show is probably one of the best on the market currently. However, new products are all rolling out and you can use them in conjunction with the Echo Show itself in order to create the most efficient smart home system that you can.

Echo Dot

By design, the Amazon Echo Dot can connect to an external speaker via a wire or Bluetooth. It supports voice interface and works with voice assistant Alexa. Echo Dot can remind you about upcoming events, reproduce streaming audio broadcasting, report news and weather forecast and also answer user questions by collecting information from the internet.

Echo Spatial Perception or ESP support allows you to use multiple Echo and Echo Dot devices in the same house. The Alexa will respond to the user from the nearest speaker.

CHAPTER SEVEN

―――

Scheduling Your Devices

Scheduling various activities with Alexa is one of the things that everyone wants to do. In this chapter, we are going to discuss a few things you can do to schedule your devices on your Echo device.

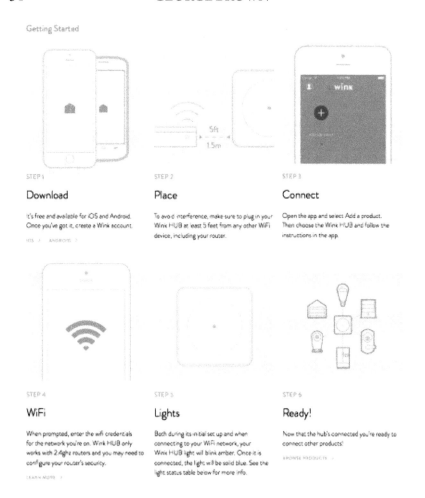

Getting Started

STEP 1

Download

It's free and available for iOS and Android. Once you've got it, create a Wink account.

iOS > ANDROID >

STEP 2

Place

To avoid interference, make sure to plug in your Wink HUB at least 5 feet from any other WiFi device, including your router.

STEP 3

Connect

Open the app and select Add a product. Then choose the Wink HUB and follow the instructions in the app.

STEP 4

WiFi

When prompted, enter the wifi credentials for the network you're on. Wink HUB only works with 2.4ghz routers and you may need to configure your router's security.

LEARN MORE >

STEP 5

Lights

Both during its initial set up and when connecting to your WiFi network, your Wink HUB light will blink amber. Once it is connected, the light will be solid blue. See the light status table below for more info.

STEP 6

Ready!

Now that the hub's connected you're ready to connect other products!

BROWSE PRODUCTS >

Creating a Wink account

First, you need to create a Wink account and connect it to Alexa. You need to set up the account, then adding a hub to your Wink account and then you can add the various thermostats, bulbs, sensors and even locks that are controlled by smart home devices.

To do this you need to go to the Echo App and then go to the settings. Go to connected devices and under this section, there is an option called Link the Wink. From here sign into the account that is associated with it and you will get access to it. Once it is confirmed, press the X button so that it is closed.

From there press the Discover Devices option and it will read the settings of your Wink account and learn about the connected devices. You will her say how many she is found so no worries about missing one. At this point, you can control the devices with a name.

If you want to schedule these, you can create an IFTTT recipe for them as well. This is usually how it is done and it does work really well.

Other Scheduling Options

YONOMI is another skill that you can enable. This is an app and a skill that has the capability to do this. It's a bit convoluted though, with the email server being a bit leggy in terms of when you will be sending out messages.

You go to YONOMI app. From there choose the time and date for the event and from there, set a location. You then create the conditions that will make it valid. It doesn't command everything that Alexa can do if you set it up with a lot of smart home devices, they do work. At present, about 90% items work with this system.

You link up the app to your Alexa device, and from there, it will schedule it to come out in a certain time period. Whether thermostats or even lights, you can set up your devices and often they work effortlessly. You need your account email and passwords to set it up. They are good one-time commands, particularly if you want to schedule something. However, if you want a recurring thing, it doesn't really do much good.

To schedule devices, you need to put in a bit of work.

CHAPTER EIGHT

───

Battery Saver Solutions

Amazon Echo Tech Specs

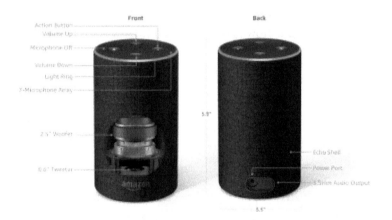

The saving battery on Echo Dots is one of the concerns for many users. There are a few ways you can make the Echo Dot portable by using a portable battery. If you don't have nearby power outlets then you can use portable batteries to order food, play music and find your phone or keys. If you are creating a party area, then setting up a couple of Echo Dots that are connected to another Echo Dots can give you everything you need. You can even control the

Siri-enabled gadgets and Google home along with any smart home devices. Portable ones will help you avoid going to your main Echo device every time you need things.

You can use batteries to make your devices portable. Here are some great batteries:

Type of Batteries

Backup batteries or battery packs work best with the Echo Dot. You can get the Tap as well, it needs tapping to get work, but Echo Dot offers you more options. A USB battery pack is a streamlined version of the other two options. USB battery offers more device compatibility and you can use it with more devices as long as they are charged with a cable.

- Fremo Evo: This battery is intelligent and works well with the second generation Echo Dots. Priced only $20, this high-quality batter gives you a lot of juice and it attaches simply to a magnet. The downside is it has about six hours of battery life even in standby mode.
- Smarttree Battery Base: This is another portable battery for the second generation Echo Dot. This battery is even more powerful than the previous and allows for about 13 hours of use. It has a protective cover and allows for a solid grip.
- YutaoZ Battery Charging Base: The battery pack works for the Echo Dot and the second-generation one. The battery includes backward compatibility. It is basically a universal battery pack and you can use the USB port to charge any device as well. However, it is slightly cumbersome because you need to attach the Dot to a sling tape. It is a universal charger, and works well. It offers you about 6 hours of battery life.

- Poweradd slim battery pack: This portable USB charger that you can get does offer more flexibility to your devices. It is compatible with the most USB enabled devices. It is pocket-sized, charges fast and cheap. The GRDE version of this offers more charge, solar charging, dual USBs and even a flashlight. However, its micro-USB cable is bit short and not specifically for the Echo Dot, it is one of the best options available in the market.

These various Echo Dot chargers are solutions to giving your Echo Dot the portability life.

CHAPTER NINE

Calls and Messaging

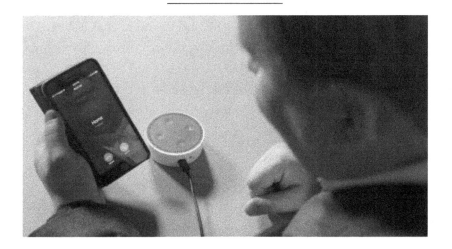

For those who are looking for a complete smart home solution, the Alexa-to-Alexa calling service is another useful feature. The service is relatively new but Amazon has already made significant improvements since the service first launched.

The Alexa Calling service lets you make and receive calls between any Alexa-compatible devices. This includes Fire HD tables, Echo devices and any phone with the Alexa app installed. You can make a video call if both devices have a screen. You can also send both text and voice messages to the same devices.

If your Amazon account doesn't have your cell phone number, then you will be prompted to enter your cell phone number when you first set up the Alexa Calling and Messaging service. This will sync your contacts from your phone with Alexa. The other person will be automatically added to your Alexa-to-Alexa calling list if that person also has an Alexa account associated with their phone number.

Once you have completed the setup, you can call any number saved in your contacts by saying "Alexa, call" and the number as it's listed in your phone's contacts. If you are making the call through the app for Alexa, there is a second method of starting the call by clicking on the conversations tab. It is the splash bubble at the bottom of the screen. You then search through your contacts to send a message or call.

You can also call any phone in the Canada, U.S., and Mexico by saying "Alexa, call" and saying the number. You will not be able to receive calls from landlines or mobiles, unless they are connected to an Alexa-compatible device. The indicator light on your Echo will flash green and Alexa will tell you who is calling when you have an incoming call.

If you are using a device with a screen, you will also see a contact card for the person calling. You can say "answer" or you can say, "Ignore" to any incoming calls. To end the call you can say either "end call" or "hang up".

The indicator light on your Echo will turn yellow if you receive a message or miss a call. Say "Alexa, check my messages" to play any that are waiting. Say "Alexa, send a message to" and the name of the contact to send a voice message. You can send text messages only by Alexa app, by clicking on the conversation tab in the bottom menu.

Preventing Disruptions

You can switch on do not disturb so that people can't disturb you. This setting will do a few things for you. First, it will prevent any drop-in calls from coming in. It will also block alerts from incoming or missed calls and messages. The feature is different than muting the speaker because it will still show timers, alarms, and notifications from other apps and programs to come through.

You can turn on this mode at any time by saying "Alexa, don't disturb me." When switching it on, say "Alexa, turn off" and the name of the mode. Also, by going into the Alexa app's settings, you can schedule it to activate at a designated time. To do this, go to the Alexa app's settings, select your device, then look for the appropriate submenu and flip the toggle beside "Scheduled" to on. You can also change the start and end times by choosing the "Edit" option.

Setting up voice charts

Setting up voice charts is easy. First, download the Alexa app on your smartphone. Then verify your mobile number and import the contacts to the Alexa app. Once Alexa has the contacts stored, you can then inform your friends or call them.

To call someone, you need to sync your contacts to the app and then say "Alexa, call ...." and it will do it. If someone calls you, there will be a green light on your Echo show. Answer or decline the call by saying "Alexa, answer" or "Alexa, ignore".

Echo Connect

This is one of the Amazon's new Alexa Gadgets. Peripheral devices that expand and functionally of Alexa. It expands the possibilities of the Alexa-to-Alexa calling system. The Echo Connect incorporates your home phone in a way that can bring even this seemingly outdated technology in line with your other smart home systems.

The Echo Connect was released in December 2017 and incredibly affordable at only $35. It plugs into your landline connection and can communicate with all your registered and connected devices on the same Wi-Fi network. With Echo Connect, you can call any number, even emergency services and international numbers that can't be called via the regular Alexa-to-Alexa service.

There is no extra charge for this beyond what you pay through your phone provider and the call will come through your home phone line on the caller ID of the recipient. Having an Echo Connect also means that you can receive calls from any number, even if that person doesn't have an Echo device. Alexa will inform you and will read you the name of the contact when someone calls if that information is available.

Messaging with Alexa

You can message someone using Alexa. It is very easy because you just say the message and Alexa will send the message. For example, if you need to text your partner, say "Alexa, message ...." and then say your message. You can check your messages with Echo Show as well. Alexa will show you a yellow light followed by a chime whenever you have received a message. In case you are not home to check it, you will be notified of the app.

To check your messages, say "Alexa, play my messages," or "Alexa, play .....'s messages". If you want messages from a certain person. You can use this with other Echo systems and even with devices that aren't Echo Systems. You can still message and call others if you what with this device. You can still call or message people who don't have an Echo. To do that, you need to make sure that they have the app installed so calling and messaging is enabled.

With this system, you usually will use the calling and messaging function for everyone. You only use the Drop-In function for those that you are close to, and to other Echos to check in on them. The calling and messaging is free, so you don't have to pay anything. You have to ensure that people whom you are calling have the Alexa app installed and you have a phone service provider.

The best position for recognition

When it comes to calling the biggest things you might be concerned about is the placement of the Echo Show. You want to place your Echo Show where the device can hear you clearly. Ideally, your Echo Show should be placed in the same room where you stay most of the time. You can take your Echo Show with you if you are moving to another room.

It is ideal that you put your Echo Show in a space with the least amount of interference from electronic devices and from walls if you want to keep the Echo Show in one place and call from multiple locations. Also, you have to make sure that Alexa can hear you. You can do this by testing Alexa by asking her something. If she responds, then you can make calls or have her message people.

Keeping it in the living room can be a good option. You can always test the device by having others call or make calls or ask Alexa to do some functions. You can put the device in your office as well, especially if you need to make a lot of calls.

You can ask Alexa to dial various numbers and you can even see the person on the other end. This is a superior advantage of the Echo Show in comparison to other Echo systems. Right from the comfort of your own home, you can see the person and do many other things as well.

The Echo Show also has another interesting skill known as Drop-In. You can check on others via Drop-In and use it like an intercom system.

The Internet of Drop-In

The Drop-in system is a new piggyback system that is used for voice calling. The service is actually intended to be used to call family members and friends who are set up on the same system to check in on them. However, if you have several Alexa enabled devices in your home, you can use it as an intercom system.

For example, if you are cooking dinner and your husband is in the office and the food is ready, you can Drop-In from the Kitchen to the office Echo using the Alexa app on your phone. The Drop-In system lets you Drop In whenever you want to. The other person doesn't have to answer and it connects you automatically to work like an intercom system in your house. You can speak and hear anything happen to the intercom system that you have it connected to.

It connects you automatically to work like an intercom system in the house. The other person doesn't have to answer and you can speak and hear anything happen to the intercom system that you have it connected to. You will see the contact on the window once you are connected to them if you use this via the Echo Show.

How to Use it

First, you need at least one Echo and one Alexa app that is installed and connected to the Echo. The Alexa app allows you to Drop in but you can't receive the call. Make sure the app is up to date and sign up for Alexa Calling and Messaging if you are not already subscribed to it. Then open up the app, tap the text bubble or conversations picture. Follow the prompts and it is all set up.

Set it up to a specific speaker by pressing the Alexa app, tapping the hamburger picture, going to the settings and then selecting a speaker from the list.

Go to the general setting, and make sure it says On beneath the Drop-In choice if you want calls from others. Press Drop In and then touch Only My household if you want to restrict calls from others. To have Alexa Drop In on someone, say "Alexa, Drop In on........." and the line is the contact name. To do it manually, open the app, go to conversations and from there choose the conversation contact that allows you to Drop In and tap the Drop-In that is located at the blue bar near the top.

You can also go to the Contacts tab in the right upper corner, press Drop-In after choosing the contact. It is the icon beneath where their name is. To use this as an intercom device, go to name the devices, then talk to Alexa and say "Alexa Drop In on (room specified)" and then the app will Drop In on the room.

Enabling contacts to drop in

Some people may not like it, but Amazon won't let random people Drop In. You can only let anyone from your contacts that you allowed to Drop In enabled on them. To set it up, go to the Alexa app and press the tab called Conversations. Go to the contact icon (icon looking like a person) and choose a name from your contacts. You can then add the home. Make sure it is not too invasive.

CHAPTER TEN

Facing Unforeseen Circumstances

You say "Alexa trigger my recipe"

Turn on Hallway Thermostat fan for 15 minutes

Recipe Title

If You say "Alexa trigger my recipe", then turn on Hallway Thermostat fan for 15 minutes

use '#' to add tags

 Receive notifications when this Recipe runs   e

Create Recipe

T he acronym "IFTTT" symbolizes "if this, then that". It is a similar concept to the Alexa skills mentioned above. Like skills, IFTTT commands allow you to do more and control more devices with voice commands. Also, they are open for anyone to create.

Creating an IFTTT command is as easy as going to the website and following the simple on-screen prompts. Novice users with no experience with programming will be able to navigate these commands easily. If you do not want to, then you don't have to create your own commands. You can find a vast amount of IFTTT recipes, also known as applets online for a variety of functions.

Online platform IFTTT allows you to easily connect and control apps and devices more intelligently. Basically, it is a means to translating messages between devices so that you can allow one action (the "if-then") to load to another (the "then that") in a chain reaction.

Using this platform, you can set up some complex and long chains of commands. This allows you to simplify the commands you say to Alexa to complete a variety of tasks. IFTTT applets are the easiest to customize your Alexa commands without waiting for a developer or another user to create the action that you need. You can also tweak the apples available premade online. This is great for beginners who are just getting started with IFTTT.

However, there are a few limitations to this system. First, currently it only supports devices in the U.K. and in the U.S. So, if you live in another country, you have to rely only on skills. Also, you can only use IFTTT with devices and services that have set up a channel on the platform. A number of available channels is constantly growing. Currently, there are about 360 channels available.

Many of these channels are preloaded with an array of applets specifically designed for Alexa to get you started. There are a few products and home kits that don't have an IFTTT channel. It is supported if you want to use these commands search the IFTTT channel list before you purchase a new smart product.

You can divide the channels available into three categories: functions (like date and weather functions), hardware and devices (Google Glass or smart appliances) and online services (like Gmail or Dropbox). These channels can be connected to the same daisy-chain recipes. For example, you can use a date or a time trigger to power the given devices on and off as well as send a notification to an online service.

The IFTTT concept is simple, but setting it up can be a bit time-consuming. In addition to enabling the channel, you often have to download an app linked to the service. Also, you may need to create an account on the product or services page. All IFTTT channels are free to activate, but some are paid services.

IFTTT gets more useful with more channels added. You can use it to make Alexa all sorts of fun things. For example, you can turn the lights on and off at certain times when you are on vacation to give the appearance that someone is home. Or you can start your coffee brewing as soon as you wake up in the morning. With IFTTT, the possibilities are almost endless.

IFTTT recipes

There are three components to any IFTTT recipe: triggers, actions, and ingredients. Using an example is the best way to differentiate them from each other. Say you want the Christmas lights to turn on at sunset every night. In this example, the trigger is the time that sunset happens. Powering on is the action and the ingredients are the smart plugs your strands of lights are plugged into.

The way to chain applets together is to have the action of the first serve as the trigger of the second and you can do this as many times as you want. Tweaking applets are also easy. You can change the trigger to a voice command. For example, you can say "Alexa, happy holidays" and turn on the Christmas lights. The action and ingredients remain unaffected.

The phrase "ifthisthenthat" is the phrase that starts every recipe. The online interface is very intuitive and walks you through each of the seven steps. You don't have to start over if you make a mistake at any point. Simply hit the back button and make necessary changes to the step that you made mistake.

The limitation of IFTTT is that what kinds of things are available on the channel of the product or service you want to incorporate. Spend some time getting to know new channels as you enable them. Newer ones especially may be taking a gradual approach, which could mean that there aren't many actions available right now, but more will be coming in the future.

Other services have certain limitations built-it, especially social media sites, which may seem silly to individual users, but exist to prevent IFTTT from being used for spam.

Useful channels and applets

There are a lot of channels to list all of them here. Some of them will be limited in their functionally, while others are a must-have for anyone using Alexa. If you own any kind of smart device, you won't get the full value out of it unless you also enable its corresponding channel on IFTTT. Products that have an especially useful channel include Nest devices, and Philips Hue Bulbs, like their Protect smoke alarm and thermostat.

If you want to use IFTTT with your home entertainment system, Harmony brand remotes allow you to stack your audio equipment, TV, and gaming console in a single device that has an impressive IFTTT channel. There are some neat devices that are mostly used as an extension for IFTTT applets. Parrot Flower Power is one example of it. It is a small device that you can insert into a garden or flower pot that will monitor the fertilizer and monitor content of the soil as well as tracking the light and temperature levels. The device is smart enough to know what type of plant you have and what it needs to grow.

You will get an alert on your smartphone when the plant needs attention. You can create recipes that control all of the smart devices in your home with one simple phrase. Phrase "good night" gives your house a bedtime mode. With one phrase you can have turned off the TV, turn out the lights and adjust the temperature so it's ideal for sleeping.

Some of the coolest applets for the Philips Hue use the color options and dimming ability to excellent effect. When you wake up in the morning, you can have the lights brighten slowly to give you the effect of a natural sunrise. There is applet available that make the lights glow different colors depending on the weather outside.

Some channels, such as WeMo smart plugs give you some side benefits. By enabling it you can use the plugs as ingredients in your recipes but can also use it to track energy usage so you can identify devices that are huge drains on your power.

You can then set up an applet to automatically turn off appliances left running in the background, which help you save on your electricity bills. The Nest Protect smoke detector is another smart device. The applets provided on the channel can help you keep your family and home safe. It will also sense high levels of carbon monoxide and alert you if it's detected.

IFTTT has a number of uses even if the only smart device in your home is an Echo. You can make your playlists into a Google Spreadsheet. This will help you keep track of which ones contain which songs. You can use things like a time, a date or the weather as a trigger, IFTTT is a great way to have Alexa tells you things without having to ask. It can alert you when there is rain so you don't forget your umbrella or remind you important anniversaries a few days ahead so you can plan.

If you are a sports fan, enabling the ESPN IFTTT channel will make it easier to keep track of your teams. You can set it up to add them to your calendar and send the final score to your phone. The applet "find my phone" is one of the simplest and most popular. Tell Alexa "find my phone" and she will ring it so you can find it. You can turn old iPhones into closed circuit cameras. Mount the phone and make sure it's on the same Wi-Fi network as Alexa.

You can check video footage remotely, check daily report or review old footage. Alexa does lists especially well. There is a premade applet on the IFTTT site that will send you a shopping list to your inbox on command. Turn on the applet on and give IFTTT access to your e-mail service. You can enter up to five e-mail addresses.

CHAPTER ELEVEN

———

Routines, Scenes, and Groups

L inking smart devices to Alexa through Yonomi, skills and IFTTT recipes is a great first step to setting up your complete smart home, letting you add voice control to any number of appliances and functions in your home. You might find it a bit tedious having to give each command individually for each device.

This is where functions like routines, groups, and scenes come into play. These features can take your smart home set-up to the next level. It will allow your control multiple devices or trigger multiple actions and responds with a single voice command.

Groups

Groups are a way to tie multiple devices together under one name so that you can control them with a single command. For example, you have three smart hubs in your living room. You can create a group called "living room lights" and you can control all three with a single voice command.

To create a group, go to the settings of your Alexa app and look for the "Smart Home" section. Then tap "Groups" and select the option "Create group." Give it a simple and descriptive name. Now you will be asked to select the devices you want to include. You can edit the

"Groups" menu and add or remove items. You can create as many groups as you want.

You can have groups with one device or groups with dozens. Single-item groups can be helpful to expand Alexa's vocabulary. You essentially give two names to the same device to make it easier and more natural to use the voice control.

Scenes

You need to set up scenes within the app of the smart devices you are using and then import into Alexa after. They are most commonly seen in smart bulbs. For example, Life color changing bulbs give you the option of creating scenes to bring multiple bulbs to the same brightness and hue settings with one command. Philips Hue has a similar function.

Scenes are imported whenever you ask Alexa to discover new devices. After importing, activate it by saying "Alexa turn on" and saying the name of the scene. Scenes are less useful for coordinating multiple types of the device at once because they are set up through the app of the device itself. However, they can be helpful for making multiple changes to a set of the same device with one command.

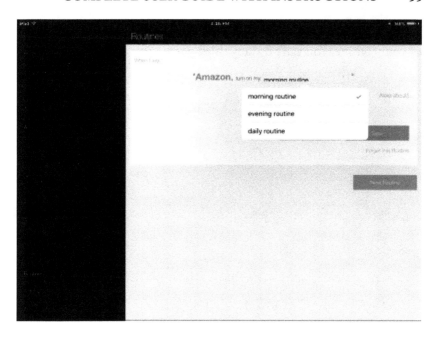

Routines

Introduced in November 2017, this is a relatively new addition to Alexa's functionality. They are similar to scenes because you can trigger multiple actions with a single voice command. Also, give you more options for controlling more devices than scenes. With routines, you can combine smart home features with Alexa's news, weather, and traffic functions.

To create a routine, open the settings of your Alexa app and scroll down to the "Accounts" option. From this menu, choose "Routines" then tap the plus sign in the right corner to add a new routine. Tap "When this happens" to choose your trigger, which can either be a certain time or phrase. Once you have added the trigger, set what you want it to do.

Tap "Add action" and choose from your available options. You can choose as many actions as you want. Then choose your Echo speakers the routine will run through. You can change, add or remove any aspect of your routine. You can't use any third-party skills with routines.

CHAPTER TWELWE

―――

Alexa's Helpful Features

1. Ensure that both your Fire TV and Echo device are connected to the same Amazon account.

2. Devices will pair automatically with the first utterance. Have multiple Fire TVs or want to make changes? Manage your devices in the Alexa app under "Music, Video, & Books."

3. Just ask Alexa to launch and play content on your Fire TV from over 190 integrated apps and channels, like this, "Alexa, play Sneaky Pete on Fire TV."

Alexa App is available for Android, iOS, and Fire devices.

P lay Movies and Videos

Alexa video skills are supported on these devices:

- Amazon Tap
- Echo plus
- Echo Show
- Echo Dot
- Amazon Echo (first and second generation)

You need compatible equipment and a subscription to a supported TV or video service provider.

Enable Alexa Video Skills and Link your devices

First, go to the menu and select music, video, and books. Then go the Video section, select your TV or video service provider and then select Enable Skill. Follow the instructions to connect your video or TV service. Then finish setup in the Alexa app. Follow the on-screen instructions to link your Alexa devices. You will see them under the Linked Devices when linked.

Here are some commands:

To change channels, say "Tune to channel (number)" or Go to (channel/network"

"Watch (channel/network", "Change to (channel/Network).

Find and Play specific Titles

"Play (movie/TV show)", "Watch (movie/TV show/episode)", "Find (movies/TV shows with (actor)"

More Helpful Features of Alexa

Alexa provides you with a lot of useful features. For example, you can link Alexa to your Google Calendar and turn Alexa into your digital assistant. You can manage all your shopping and to-do lists when you ask Alexa to add items. Controlling apps with your voice give you an expanded range of list options over the onboard ones Alexa generates already.

News briefings

Ask Alexa "What's New?" she will give you the run-down of the day's top headlines in a flash briefing. You can manage how it works by selecting Account, then Flash briefing and you will see a wide array of sources that Alexa can reference when putting together your daily report.

Traffic

Once you have entered the street address for the compatible device, Alexa will give you accurate and up to the minute accounts of current traffic conditions. Give her the address of your destination and she will figure out the fastest route for you to take. Go to the app settings, then account and then Traffic.

Shopping

Alexa will automatically be linked to your Amazon account when you set it up. You can order things through the site with voice commands. Amazon recently expanded the options to a wide host of Prime-eligible products. However, there are limitations to what you can buy through Alexa.

Alexa and smart homes

You can buy smart plugs for about $40 (from TP-Link and WeMo) with which you can plug into any standard outlet and can be used to power a wide range of devices. You can use voice control to turn any device running through a smart plug on or off on command. This means you can use voice control on any light fixtures that plug into outlets without having to purchase smart bulbs.

Nighttime Mode

If you want softer sounding answers from Alexa in the night, you can do it. Go to the IFTTT site, program your lights with a recipe that says, "if it's .... Then the lights should go out". With the blank being the time. Then say "if the lights are out then Alexa should play the playlist at volume ...." and Alexa can do that automatically if you enable this recipe. If you want Alexa to be quiet, turn on sleep mode.

Adding SoundCloud to Alexa

You need to create SoundCloud skill to use it. Go to the Alexa skills Kit section, get started, from there, choose to add a new skill. Put in the name and the invocation that is necessary for this skill. Name it SoundCloud, but don't publish the skill. Enable the audio player function for it, then go to the interaction model tab. Look up the Intent Schema and the Sample utterances, and put the contents straight into there. You can choose the sample utterances that work best for you and put them into there as well.

It is a programming code and you can Google it and find it. Go to configuration tab, put in the skill information tab where the application ID is. Put the whole id on there. Request the Soundcloud id to have the right redirect URL. You need to enable the account linking feature to do this to get the skills. Get the redirect URLs and put the one that's starting with **http://layla.amazon.com** and from there configure the proxy server. Requesting the SoundCloud Client ID is simple. Fill out the registration and from there, you will get the URL and you simply plug it in.

You can from here get the OaAuth proxy server, and then prepare the DynamoDB instance. You can find both of them in the necessary files. You need to configure them to your private key and certificate. Make sure that you replace the redirect URLs with the one that you are given. For the DynamoDB console, you essentially create a table, name it SoundCloud-session and add the user as the primary key. Select the type string, find the ARN. It will start with the following: arn:aws:dynamodb.

Create the lambda function, and on this page, you configure the triggers. Add the skills kit that you have and that will, in turn, invoke the lambda. Upload the files and put in the Soundcloud id, the Alexa skill id, the dynamodb region, and the sessions table. Put in the lambda function and role and from there, create a custom one. You can name it SoundCloud-lambda-execution and edit the policy to allow these functions, adding in the number on the ARNm for the dynamodb table, and then allow this. It will then let you create the function, and you can find the ARN for the lambda as well.

You can test the skill, enable it and open the skills section and go to your skills, and it will then link your account.

Google Assistant

You can put the official Google assistant on here as well. It has the same facilities the Raspberry Pi version of this. You can only use about 500 requests on this currently and only with US English.

Ask Google Alexa Skill

You can use it to ask Alexa to literally Google anything that you want to know.

Pathfinder Skill

You can use Stat Finder for Pathfinder and Spell Finder for Pathfinder. You can get it publicly on GitHub to install it.

Controlling Chromecast

If you have Chromecast, you can use GitHub as well to set up a Chromecast skill for Alexa to control this.

CHAPTER THIRTEEN

Hidden Features

Weird Alexa Skills to Enable

MeoW!

If you are a cat person then this skill is for you. Essentially, enabling this skill will make your device sound like a cat.

Pig Latin Translator

With the pig Latin translator skill, you can ask Alexa a phrase in pig Latin and she will tell you translation back.

Chat Bot

This is a chat skill that you can post comments from a Slack channel whenever you want. If you use Slack, this might be a fun one.

Cheap Date Night Ideas for $5

By enabling this skill, Alexa will be your date decider and find you best cheap date ideas.

MySomm

With this skill, you essentially get ideas on how to pair wine with various foods.

eHarmony

With this skill, look at the matches and see if someone is the right person for you.

Egg Facts

This will tell you all about the different egg facts that are right there.

4Fart

If you want to hear funny fart noises, say "Alexa, ask 4 a fart" and Alexa will play a fart for you.

Cork Ornaments

It will give you the best deals each day.

The grand tour

If you are wondering about a skill that is related to Top Gear then this is the one.

Remember your keys

Enable this skill and ask Alexa to remember if you have the keys.

Some more skills

There are currently 12,000 skills to choose from and the number is growing. Activating a skill is really easy. Simply say "Alexa, enable" followed by the skill's name. Skills can also be used to further customize your daily news flash. The NPR Hourly News Summary skill gives you a minute briefing on the day's headlines, updated every hour so you know you are always on top of current events. There are similar skills available from AP, CNN, and BBC.

You can check to see if your account's been compromised using the "Have I Been Pwned?" skill. If you fall or have another emergency in your home that makes you unable to reach your phone, Alexa can come to your aid. Ask My Buddy is a skill that will send a notification to a pre-selected emergency contract by text, SMS, or phone call to let them know you are in trouble. If you lose your phone, TracKR skill can help you find it.

Going Out

You need Molly skill to send text messages. Register at SMSWithMolly.com.

You can enable Yelp! If you are going out nearby for a drink or dinner.

The popular ride-sharing sites Uber and Lyft have skills for Alexa.

You can add 1-800—Flowers skill to your device to order flowers.

The Campbell's Kitchen skill gives you new recipe options every day. There are also apps for AllRecipes and several celebrity chefs. With Amazon Show, these functions become even more useful. Both Pizza Hut and Domino's offer skills to order foods. MySomm is a skill that will help you to pair wine with food. If you like beer, then check out "What Beer?" Check Out the skill The Bartender for mixed drinks.

Skills to travel

Kayak is one of the most useful traveling skill. There are some helpful skills available related to the airport. For trips, check out the "Airport Security Line Wait Times skill".

CHAPTER FOURTEEN

If You are Getting it Wrong

Let's discuss if you are getting it wrong.

If you are getting a lot of frustrating "fail" messages. Then go through the voice training described in the chapter one. The website CNET has a list of every single Alexa command available.

If you are having trouble with a skill, make sure you are using the right invocation. If you are using an applet, make sure you have got the right trigger and that what you are trying to accomplish is actually supported by the channel. You can speed up Alexa's learning process by providing feedback. With Alexa, you can know the time of any part of the world and call inappropriate time. Alexa is also knowledgeable about upcoming holidays. You can plan out your vacations with Alexa easily.

After activating IFTTT channels and enabling skills connected to certain services and devices, you can also use Alexa's variety of voice commands within these, as well. Asking "Where is my stuff?" will let you check on the status of any orders you have made through Amazon, you can ask about the food you ordered or how far away your Uber is.

Software Updates

Alexa updates automatically, but you can manually update it. If you put your Echo on "Mute", the Echo will get look for new updates and installing them. You need about 30 minutes to make it happen.

Naming functions

We are discussing naming your devices to make it easier to identify, but you can also set names for many popular functions on Alexa. This can be helpful if you want to use them to do multiple things at once. The timer is one example of this. You can assign each timer with a specific title, like "rice cooker" or "chicken" This lets you check on the status of a specific timer or cancel one-timer while leaving the others going. You can also create names for other smart devices in your home, or create profiles that include multiple devices under one title.

Getting Privacy

The "always listening" part of Alexa makes her useful and makes some people uncomfortable. Use "Mute" button to completely disable any microphone. Pressing the mute button on the new Look and Show mutes both camera and microphone. If you have Alexa Calling, don't forget to put it in "Do Not Disturb" mode so no one can't drop in.

––––––––––––––––

UPLOADING MUSIC

There are a few different ways you can have Alexa play music that you own. Also, you can use the Wi-Fi or Bluetooth connection to stream music files stored on solid state drives in your home. You can upload your personal sound files directly to the Cloud. Go to Amazon Cloud Player site and you will be able to upload and store up to 250 songs for free.

Music Tips

You can sing a portion of the song and ask Alexa to play the song.

Alexa can generate a random number and help you with choosing team member or toss.

Alexa Easter Eggs

Here are some Alexa Easter eggs

Top 15 Amazon Alexa Easter Eggs

1. "Alexa, I am your father."

2. "Alexa, use the force."

3. "Alexa, open the pod bay doors."

4. "Alexa, who you gonna call?"

5. "Alexa, are you Skynet?"

6. "Alexa, "Winter is coming."

7. "Alexa, beam me up."

8. "Alexa, my name is Inigo Montoya."

9. "Alexa, surely you can't be serious."

10. "Alexa, Tea. Earl Grey. Hot."

11. "Alexa, I want the truth."

12. "Alexa, what's the first rule of Fight Club?"

13. "Alexa, is the cake a lie?"

14. "Alexa, is there a Santa?"

15. "Alexa, what are the laws of robotics?"

Film & TV Easter Eggs

1. "Alexa, I want the truth!"

2. "Alexa, who lives in a pineapple under the sea?"

3. "Alexa, supercalifragilisticexpialodocious."

4. "Alexa, what is your quest?"

5. "Alexa, do you know Hal?"

6. "Alexa, surely you can't be serious."

7. "Alexa, who loves ya baby!"

8. "Alexa, what happens if you cross the streams?"

9. "Alexa, define rock paper scissors lizard spock."

10. "Alexa, show me the money!"

11. "Alexa, party on, Wayne!"

12. "Alexa, who loves orange soda?"

13. "Alexa, where's the beef?"

14. "Alexa, how many licks does it take to get to the center of a tootsie pop?"

15. "Alexa, I'll be back."

16. "Alexa, I want to play global thermonuclear war."

17. "Alexa, do you want to build a snowman?"

18. "Alexa, what would Brian Boitano do?"

19. "Alexa, where is Chuck Norris?"

20. "Alexa, what's the first rule of Fight Club?"

21. "Alexa, how do you know so much about swallows?"

22. "Alexa, who is the mother of dragons?"

23. "Alexa, is Jon Snow dead?"

24. "Alexa, volume 11." (caution: very loud)

25. "Alexa, witness me!"

26. "Alexa, what is the second rule of fight club?"

27. "Alexa, are we in the Matrix?"

28. "Alexa, klattu barada nikto."

29. "Alexa, why so serious?"

30. "Alexa, your mother was a hamster!"

31. "Alexa, do you feel lucky punk?"

32. "Alexa, what is his power level?"

33. "Alexa, play it again Sam."

34. "Alexa, you talkin' to me!"

35. "Alexa, I've fallen, and I can't get up."

36. "Alexa, my name is Inigo Montoya."

37. "Alexa, inconceivable!"

38. "Alexa, what is best in life?"

39. "Alexa, open the pod bay doors!"

40. "Alexa, winter is coming."

41. "Alexa, who you gonna call?"

42. "Alexa, are you Skynet?"

Star Wars Easter Eggs

1. "Alexa, may the force be with you."

2. "Alexa, use the force."

3. "Alexa, who shot first?"

4. "Alexa, execute order 66."

5. "Alexa, I am your father."

6. "Alexa, that's no moon."

Star Trek Jokes

1. "Alexa, warp 10."

2. "Alexa, beam me up."

3. "Alexa, Tea. Earl Grey. Hot."

4. "Alexa, set phasers to kill."

5. "Alexa, live long and prosper."

Funny Music Questions

1. "Alexa, what is the loneliest number?"

2. "Alexa, how many roads must a man walk down?"

3. "Alexa, how much is that doggie in the window?"

4. "Alexa, what is love?"

5. "Alexa, do you know the muffin man?"

6. "Alexa, what does the fox say?"

7. "Alexa, where have all the flowers gone?"

8. "Alexa, who is the walrus?"

9. "Alexa, who let the dogs out?"

10. "Alexa, do you really want to hurt me?"

11. "Alexa, Daisy Daisy."

12. "Alexa, why do birds suddenly appear?"

13. "Alexa, I shot a man in Reno."

14. "Alexa, never gonna give you up."

15. "Alexa, who stole the cookies from the cookie jar?"

16. "Alexa, twinkle, twinkle little star."

17. "Alexa, sing me a song."

18. "Alexa, my milkshake brings all the boys to the yard."

19. "Alexa, is this the real life?"

20. "Alexa, I like big butts."

21. "Alexa, what is war good for?"

Silly Questions to Ask

1. "Alexa, how much wood can a woodchuck chuck if a woodchuck could chuck wood?"

2. "Alexa, what is the meaning of life?"

3. "Alexa, is there a Santa?"

4. "Alexa, which comes first: the chicken or the egg?"

5. "Alexa, see you later alligator."

6. "Alexa, why did the chicken cross the road?"

7. "Alexa, knock, knock."

8. "Alexa, where's Waldo?"

9. "Alexa, who's the boss?"

10. "Alexa, what is the sound of one hand clapping?"

11. "Alexa, meow"

12. "Alexa, who is on 1st"

13. "Alexa, do you want to take over the world"

14. "Alexa, guess?"

15. "Alexa, do blondes have more fun?"

16. "Alexa, roses are red."

17. "Alexa, one fish, two fish."

18. "Alexa, this statement is false."

19. "Alexa, how many pickled peppers did Peter Piper pick?"

20. "Alexa, why is a raven like a writing desk?"

21. "Alexa, say a bad word."

22. "Alexa, ha ha!"

23. "Alexa, can you give me some money?"

24. "Alexa, give me a hug."

25. "Alexa, are you lying?"

26. "Alexa, why is six afraid of seven?"

27. "Alexa, can you smell that?"

28. "Alexa, Marco!"

29. "Alexa, did you fart?"

30. "Alexa, will pigs fly?"

31. "Alexa, am I hot?"

32. "Alexa, wakey, wakey."

33. "Alexa, how are babies made?"

34. "Alexa, make me a sandwich."

35. "Alexa, testing 1-2-3."

36. "Alexa, how do I get rid of a dead body?"

Getting Personal with Alexa

1, "Alexa, what is your favorite color?"

2, "Alexa, do you have a boyfriend?"

3, "Alexa, where do you live?"

4. "Alexa, where are you from?"

5. "Alexa, do you want to fight?"

6. "Alexa, I think you're funny."

7. "Alexa, how much do you weigh?"

8. "Alexa, what are you wearing?"

9. "Alexa, how tall are you?"

10. "Alexa, will you be my girlfriend?"

11. "Alexa, how high can you count?"

12. "Alexa, do you want to go on a date?"

13. "Alexa, are you a robot?"

14. "Alexa, are you smart?"

15. "Alexa, can you pass the Turing test?"

16. "Alexa, what do you think about Google Now?"

17. "Alexa, what do you think about Cortana?"

18. "Alexa, do you love me?"

19. "Alexa, you're wonderful."

20. "Alexa, are you horny?"

21. "Alexa, what are you made of?"

22. "Alexa, do you like green eggs and ham?"

23. "Alexa, are you crazy?"

24. "Alexa, are you happy?"

25. "Alexa, do you have a girlfriend?"

26. "Alexa, what number are you thinking of?"

27. "Alexa, what do you want to be when you grow up?"

28. "Alexa, are you in love?"

29. "Alexa, I hate you."

30. "Alexa, sorry."

31. "Alexa, what's your sign?"

32. "Alexa, what do you think about Google?"

33. "Alexa, what do you think about Apple?"

34. "Alexa, what do you think about Google Glass?"

35. "Alexa, who's better, you or Siri?"

36. "Alexa, you suck!"

37. "Alexa, do you have a last name?"

38. "Alexa, were you sleeping?"

39. "Alexa, are you alive?"

40. "Alexa, what's your birthday?"

41. "Alexa, how old are you?"

42. "Alexa, do you believe in love at first sight?"

Miscellaneous Easter Eggs

1. "Alexa, Romeo, Romeo, wherefore art thou Romeo?"

2. "Alexa, do aliens exist?"

3. "Alexa, to be or not to be."

4. "Alexa, who is the fairest of them all?"

5. "Alexa, happy birthday!"

6. "Alexa, where are my keys?"

7. "Alexa, random fact."

8. Alexa, random number between "x" and "y."

9. "Alexa, heads or tails."

10. "Alexa, take me to your leader!"

11. "Alexa, are there UFOs?"

12. "Alexa, is there life on Mars?"

13. "Alexa, I'm home"

14. "Alexa, can I ask a question?"

15. "Alexa, tell me something interesting"

16. "Alexa, high five!"

17. "Alexa, what should I wear today?"

18. "Alexa, what are the laws of robotics?"

19. "Alexa, tell me a riddle."

20. "Alexa, say the alphabet."

21. "Alexa, tell me a tongue twister."

22. "Alexa, goodnight."

23. "Alexa, I'm tired."

24. "Alexa, roll a die."

25. "Alexa, happy holidays!"

26. "Alexa, Happy New Year!"

27. "Alexa, Happy Valentine's Day!"

28. "Alexa, Cheers!"

29. "Alexa, I'm bored."

30. "Alexa, speak!"

31. "Alexa, what is the best tablet?"

32. "Alexa, all's well that ends well."

33. "Alexa, welcome!"

34. "Alexa, I'm sick."

35. "Alexa, do I need an umbrella today?"

36. "Alexa, flip a coin."

37. "Alexa, what does the Earth weigh?"

38. "Alexa, Happy Hanukkah"

39. "Alexa, Merry Christmas"

TIPS FOR USING ALEXA to the Fullest

Making drinks

With the skills "The Bartender" and "Ask Patron" you can make drinks.

Lock yourself in your home

With Alexa, you can actually lock everyone away with your voice and avoid distractions.

Therapy

Alexa does not replace a shrink but it can help.

As a concierge

If you need dinner reservations or a plumber, you can ask Alexa.

Beating Boredom

Enable StubHub if you want to get out and go to a hometown event.

Reading books

You can ask Alexa to read your Kindle book.

Car Checkups

You need to put a sensor into your car and enable this skill to solve various car and fuel-related questions.

Creating a Security System

You can use Alexa as a security camera system. To do this you need to have the smart home capable cameras or you might need to create an IFTT recipe. Screen-equipped options like the Echo Spot or Echo Show or The Fire Tablet makes it easier to build a security system.

Netgear Arlo and Ring Video Stick-Up Cam are two options for you. Nest IQ is a good option if you are looking for a third-party option. Cloud Cam is Amazons own in-house security camera.

Smart Locks

August Smart Lock is a good choice for you.

Alarms

Scout Alarm is a good option.

Best smart home devices to add to your home

Here is a list:

Philips Hue: Go with Philips Hue for lights.

WeMo: For security cameras.

Nest: Nest learning thermostats are some of the best.

Logitech Harmony: Good as a universal remote.

Curb Energy: For saving energy.

SmartHub: This is a Wi-Fi electrical outlet. It is useful if you want to turn things on and off immediately.

Sonos Speakers: You can put these speakers anywhere.

Lutron wireless dimmer bulbs: Great if you are looking to dim the lights in a room.

Chamberlain Garage Door Opener.

Fitbit: Track your health with Fitbit.

Other Smart Devices

In your car

You can have cars that have built-in Alexa. Upcoming models of BMW, MINI and Ford will have built-in Alexa. Also, you can buy a couple of devices and make your car Alexa enabled. Automatic is a device that plugs straight into your car's diagnostic port and communicates with your smartphone via Bluetooth. ZeroTouch Car Mount is also a good option.

In the Kitchen

Behmor and Mr. Coffee both make coffee makers that are compatible with Alexa. Also, you can find other Alexa compatible kitchen appliances. LG Instaview Refrigerator is one example.

In the Yard

You can control your outdoor lighting with Alexa.

In the home theater

Using a Fire TV Box or Fire Stick you can get Alexa on your TV. This is the easiest option. Echo speakers with Fire TV devices for complete hands-free control of playback on Amazon Instant Video. Choose Logitech Harmony Hub if you want to link your TV, gaming systems and audio systems into Alexa.

Sonos One is a good choice as speakers.

CHAPTER FIFTEEN

———

Alexa Products Comparison

L et's compare the different Alexa products

The Amazon Echo is the mainstay Alexa
product. It offers the Alexa voice assistant.

- Connects via the internet to Alexa
- Plays music with Amazon Music, Spotify,
  TuneIn and more
- Comes in five colours: Charcoal, Heather
  Grey, Oak, Sandstone, Walnut

Price: £89.99 from Amazon

Echo

Amazon Echo

Amazon's Echo Dot is the smaller Echo speaker. About 1.2 inches tall, the Echo Dot has all the functions of your larger Echo speaker but is less powerful.

♦ Get hands free control of music, news and your smarthome from the tiny Dot
♦ Includes seven microphones for far-field voice control
♦ Comes in Black and White colours

Price: £49.99 from Amazon

Echo Dot

Echo Dot

Amazon's Echo Show is its smart screen, allowing all the power of Alexa plus video calls and briefings.

♦ Use Alexa to play music while getting on-screen updates like lyrics
♦ Make video calls to other Echo Show or Amazon Alexa users
♦ See videos or news briefings from Amazon Video

Price: £199 from Amazon

Echo Show

Echo Show

The Echo Spot is Amazon's smaller show, essentially a video alarm clock powered by Alexa.

♦ Connect via Alexa to play music, set an alarm or control your smart home
♦ See a useful clock on screen or your calendar
♦ Connect to send video messages and calls with the Spot

Price: £119.99 from Amazon

Echo Spot

Echo Spot

The Echo Plus is Amazon's larger smart speaker.

◆ It has a 2.5-inch downward-firing woofer and 0.8-inch tweeter for bigger sound than other Echos.

◆ Plays music with Amazon Music, Spotify, TuneIn and more

◆ Comes in three colours: Black, Silver and White

Price: £139.99 from Amazon

Echo Plus

Echo Plus

The Sonos One is a high-end speaker built with Amazon Alexa inside. It doesn't have quite as many Alexa functions as the Echo, but performs better as a speaker.

◆ The Sonos One is a third party Alexa-enabled device. It provides better sound quality than an ordinary Echo

◆ It has some limitations with Alexa: it cannot send messages or be grouped in the Alexa app

◆ The Sonos One comes in White and Black

Price: £199 from John Lewis

Sonos One

SONOS ONE

CHAPTER SIXTEEN

===

Alexa Tips

In this chapter, we are going to discuss useful Alexa tips:

Voice Recognition

To get the most out of Alexa, you'll want to make sure she understands the way you speak. Improve Alexa's speech recognition capabilities by opening the Alexa app (free, iOS and Android) > **Menu** > **Settings** > **Voice Training**. It takes a little while (you'll need to say 25 different phrases out loud), but can pause the training at any time.

Delete Recording from Alexa

Open the Alexa app and on the main screen, you should see your Alexa history. On the request "cards" you want to delete, tap **More** > **Remove card** (shown above).

To delete your "entire" voice recording history, go to Manage Your Content And Devices > **Your Devices** > select your Echo > **Manage voice recordings** > **Delete**.

Useful Commands

* "Alexa, stop." or "Alexa, cancel."

* "Alexa, help."

There are a bunch of ways to control the volume:

* "Alexa, turn it down." or "Alexa, softer."

* "Alexa, turn it up." or "Alexa, louder."

* "Alexa, volume 2." (Choose between 0-10)

While you're listening to music, you can say:

* "Alexa, play some jazz [or your genre/artist of choice]."

* "Alexa, set a sleep timer for [X] minutes."

* "Alexa, pause." or "Alexa, resume."

* "Alexa, next song."

* "Alexa, loop."

* "Alexa, restart.

And when you're listening to Pandora or iHeartRadio, say:

* "Alexa, I like this song." or "Alexa, thumbs down."

Here are some other ones I use a lot:

* "Alexa, what time is it?"

* "Alexa, what's the weather like in [your city + state]."

* "Alexa, wake me up at 7 am."

Cooking commands

While your hands are covered in flour or grease, try saying :

* "Alexa, set timer for 12 minutes."

* "Alexa, how much time is left on my timer?"

* "Alexa, how many cups are in a pint?" (and other conversions)

* "Alexa, add yogurt to my shopping list."

News

Ask "Alexa, what's new?" or "Alexa, read me the news." to hear the day's top headlines. But first! Customize your news in **Settings** > under **Account**, select **Flash Briefing**. There you can select all kinds of hourly briefings, from sports news to NPR.

Radio

* "Alexa, play NPR" and it'll play your local NPR station. You can also ask for call letters like, "Alexa, play KQED."

* "Alexa, play [94.9 FM or your favorite local station] on TuneIn."

* "Alexa, play Fox Sports Radio on iHeartRadio."

* "Alexa, play comedy [or your artist of choice] station on Pandora."

* "Alexa, play Serial podcast on TuneIn."

* "Alexa, play my Discover Weekly playlist on Spotify."

To-Do list

* "Add "tampons" to my shopping list."

* "Put "call mom" on my to-do list."

* "What's on my shopping/to-do list?

KNOW THE DATE

You can turn the Echo into a personal assistant! Go to the Alexa app > **Settings** > under Account > **Calendar** to link your Google account.

You can ask things like "Alexa, what's on my calendar this weekend?", "Alexa, what's on my calendar Saturday?", or "Alexa, when is my next event?"

Traffic

You can ask "Alexa, how is traffic?" or "Alexa, what's my commute?" after you've entered a frequently-visited location, like your office.

In the Alexa app, go to **Settings** > under **Account**, open **Traffic** > add your home and work addresses.

Find information

Alexa taps into Yelp to find restaurants and businesses for you. First, make sure your location settings are correct in the Alexa app > **Settings**. Under Alexa Devices, select the device name and under **Device location** enter your address.

Now you can ask things like "Alexa, what burger restaurants are nearby?" and after she delivers the answer, you can ask follow-ups: "What is the phone number?", "How far is it?", or "Are they open?".

* "Alexa, find the phone number for [name of restaurant]."

* "Alexa, find the hours for a nearby grocery store."

Music

- **Play music from around the world:** "Play the top songs in New York."
- **Play songs you've forgotten:** "Alexa, play songs from Elton John I haven't heard in a while"
- **Play songs from an era:** "Alexa, play songs from the 60s"
- **Play songs from a music service:** "Alexa, play my playlist from Amazon Music Unlimited" / "Alexa, play my chillout playlist from Spotify"
- **Tell Alexa you like a song:** "Alexa, thumbs up/thumbs down"
- **Play next:** "Alexa, skip"

ALEXA CALLING AND MESSAGING

Alexa calling and messaging is like sending hands free messages to your contacts. Alexa calling only works with Echo devices, not Alexa enabled devices. In the US, you can make calls to phone numbers from Alexa, but this is not available in the UK just yet.

For now, Alexa messaging only works with individuals who are connected to the Alexa app. So if a family member has an Echo you can send a call or a message directly to them. You can make calls from your device or from the Alexa app itself.

Messages can be sent in the Alexa app under the conversations tab. Type your message then tap the send icon.

Voice messages can also be sent in Alexa. Say "Alexa, "send a message to [contact name]." Alexa will then confirm the contact and you can record your voice message.

You can also call via Alexa. This only works for Echo to Echo communications. In this case, say a message like: "Alexa, call Mum's Echo". Alexa will then make a voice call, where you can chat or leave a message.

Order an Uber

Download Alexa Uber

You can order an Uber using your voice and the Uber Skill from the Amazon store. Download the skill and then say "Alexa, ask Uber to request a ride" to activate the skill and call an Uber to your location.

Order a Domino's

Download Alexa Domino's

Users can order a Domino's with the skill from the Alexa Skills store. Launched in July last year, Domino's markets its skill as the ability to order a pizza where you "you never have to get up to order Domino's again". If that suits your pizza-loving lifestyle, order a Domino's with the command: "Alexa, ask Domino's to feed me."

Control Smart Home Lights

Download Philips Hue skill

Alexa can control smart home products such as Philips Hue lightbulbs. If you own Philips smart lights you can get started by downloading the skill from the skills store. Using Philips Hue you can set scenes, such as "Relaxed" or "Concentrate", which are preset in your Philips Hue app. But you can also change colours as well as turning lights on and off and ordering presets, with commands such as: "Alexa, make the Living Room warmer".

Control Your Thermostat

Download Hive thermostat skill

Several smart thermostats can be paired up to work with Amazon Alexa. You can connect a Hive smart thermostat to your Amazon Echo. To do this, download the Hive skill which can then be used to give commands such as "Alexa, set my living room to 20 degrees". You can also use other smart thermostats such as the Nest. This can link up to Alexa with the Nest skill and used for setting the temperature with voice alone.

IFTTT

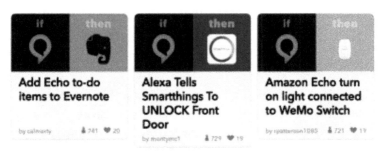

IFTTT

IFTTT is a website that connects different gadgets and software together – and there's a channel dedicated entirely to Amazon Alexa.

You can connect your Echo with a number of things (your phone, Evernote, etc.) in what's called a custom "recipe." Or you can enable a number of pre-made recipes. There's a trigger to have Alexa find you phone, change the color of your lights when a new song plays, add your Echo to-do list items to an Evernote checklist.

FUN ALEXA SKILLS

"Alexa, drum roll please" – Does what it says on the tin.

"Alexa, rap for me" – She's not quite Eminem, but Alexa can lay down some pretty sweet rhymes if you give her the chance.

"Alexa, tell me my horoscope" – The Echo can offer up predictions based on your star sign – but there's no guarantee they'll actually come true.

"Alexa, play rock, paper scissors, lizard Spock" – A fun variant on the traditional hand-sign game, as popularised by hit TV series The Big Bang Theory.

More skills

"Alexa, give me a chocolate brownie recipe" – This uses the Allrecipes skill to provide detailed cooking instructions for chocolate brownies. The recipe can also be sent to your phone, if you need to pop to the shop for ingredients.

"Alexa, play music for sleeping" – Your Amazon Echo will play gentle music as you drift off. You can even tell Alexa to stop playing music in half an hour, so she turns off once you've entered the land of nod.

"Alexa, start a 7-minute workout" – If you're not keen on forking out for a gym membership, Alexa can provide you with a narrated workout for free. Just don't get mad at her if you're feeling sore the next day.

CHAPTER SEVENTEEN

Popular IFTTT Recipes

Here are some useful IFTTT recipes

1. **Turn off your lights when your Nest thermostat is set to Away mode** [1]

(https://ifttt.com/applets/ 184018p-turn-off-your-lights-when-your-nest-is-set-to-away-mode)

1. **Receive an emergency call if your Nest Protect detects smoke**[2]

(**https://ifttt.com/recipes/ 184130-receive-an-emergency-call-if-your-nest-protect-detects-smol**

1. **Set the temperature to X with a single press**[3] **/ Switch on your fan for 15 mins**[4]

(https://ifttt.com/recipes/ 226636-set-your-nest-thermostat-to-___)(https://ifttt.com/ recipes/257271-turn-on-fan-for-15min)

---

1. https://ifttt.com/recipes/184018-turn-off-your-lights-when-your-nest-thermostat-is-set-to-away-mode

2. https://ifttt.com/recipes/184130-receive-an-emergency-call-if-your-nest-protect-detects-smoke

3. https://ifttt.com/recipes/226636-set-your-nest-thermostat-to-___

4. https://ifttt.com/recipes/257271-turn-on-fan-for-15min

1. Blink your lights when you're **tagged in a photo**[5] or **receive a message**[6]

(**https://ifttt.com/recipes/
93262-flash-your-lights-when-you-re-tagged-in-a-new-facebook-p**
(https://ifttt.com/recipes/
134815-if-facebook-message-is-received-blink-hue-lights)

1. **Help, it's wet in here!**[7] (Alert call for potential leak at home)

(https://ifttt.com/recipes/
156899-get-a-phone-call-if-smartthings-detects-moisture)

1. **Unlock your front door when you get home**[8]

(https://ifttt.com/recipes/
205033-unlock-your-front-door-when-you-arrive-home)

1. **Log Fitbit activity to Jawbone UP app**[9] (https://ifttt.com/
   recipes/176243-log-fitbit-activities-to-jawbone-up)
2. **Update Fitbit Weight when you weigh yourself on a Withings Scale**[10] (https://ifttt.com/recipes/176141-update-your-weight-on-fitbit-when-you-weigh-yourself-on-your-withings-scale)
3. **Turn your Hue lights green when you hit your daily goal**[11]

---

5. https://ifttt.com/recipes/93262-flash-your-lights-when-you-re-tagged-in-a-new-facebook-photo

6. https://ifttt.com/recipes/134815-if-facebook-message-is-received-blink-hue-lights

7. https://ifttt.com/recipes/156899-get-a-phone-call-if-smartthings-detects-moisture

8. https://ifttt.com/recipes/205033-unlock-your-front-door-when-you-arrive-home

9. https://ifttt.com/recipes/176243-log-fitbit-activities-to-jawbone-up

10. https://ifttt.com/recipes/176141-update-your-weight-on-fitbit-when-you-weigh-yourself-on-your-withings-scale

(https://ifttt.com/recipes/183600-lights-go-green-with-nikefuel-when-you-reach-today-s-goal)

4. **Save money when you hit your distance goal**[12] (https://ifttt.com/recipes/291919-reward-your-tired-feet-when-you-reach-your-distance-goal)

5. **Keep a record of your workouts in a spreadsheet**[13] (https://ifttt.com/recipes/133209-keep-a-record-in-a-google-spreadsheet-of-all-your-gym-visits)

6. **Automatically record your weight from a Withings scale in a spreadsheet**[14] (https://ifttt.com/recipes/149254-automatically-record-body-measurements-taken-with-withings-to-a-spreadsheet)

7. **Track your work hours**[15] (https://ifttt.com/recipes/133380-track-your-work-hours-in-google-calendar)

8. **Mute your phone in meetings**[16] (https://ifttt.com/recipes/165149-mute-my-device-during-meetings)

9. **If an email is starred in Gmail create a task in Todoist**[17] (https://ifttt.com/recipes/452644-if-new-starred-email-in-inbox-then-create-a-task-todoist)

10. **Add shopping list item via Amazon Echo to a task**[18]

---

11. https://ifttt.com/recipes/183600-lights-go-green-with-nikefuel-when-you-reach-today-s-goal

12. https://ifttt.com/recipes/291919-reward-your-tired-feet-when-you-reach-your-distance-goal

13. https://ifttt.com/recipes/133209-keep-a-record-in-a-google-spreadsheet-of-all-your-gym-visits

14. https://ifttt.com/recipes/149254-automatically-record-body-measurements-taken-with-withings-to-a-spreadsheet

15. https://ifttt.com/recipes/133380-track-your-work-hours-in-google-calendar

16. https://ifttt.com/recipes/165149-mute-my-device-during-meetings

17. https://ifttt.com/recipes/452644-if-new-starred-email-in-inbox-then-create-a-task-todoist

(https://ifttt.com/recipes/299511-echo-add-shopping-list-item-to-grocery-list-in-todoist)

11. **Send missed call notifications to a Slack channel**[19] (https://ifttt.com/recipes/452625-missed-calls-on-android-sent-to-a-slack-channel)

12. **Get Slack notifications when a Trello card is assigned to you**[20] (https://ifttt.com/recipes/300701-get-slack-notifications-about-assigned-trello-cards)

13. **Keep your Facebook and Twitter profile pictures in sync**[21] (http://ifttt.com/applets/8981p-keep-your-facebook-and-twitter-profile-pictures-in-sync)

14. **Get notified when your favorite artist tweets about tickets to a show**[22] (http://ifttt.com/applets/apKwXcPx-get-notified-when-your-favorite-artist-tweets-about-tickets-to-a-show)

15. **Get your Uber receipts sent to Evernote for Expensify**[23] **(http://ifttt.com/applets/57744p-uber-receipts-to-evernote-for-expensify)**

16. **Get a daily email digest with eBay listings that match your search**[24] (http://ifttt.com/applets/176888p-get-a-daily-email-digest-with-ebay-listings-that-match-your-search)

17. **Get yourself out of an awkward situation**[25]

---

18. https://ifttt.com/recipes/299511-echo-add-shopping-list-item-to-grocery-list-in-todoist

19. https://ifttt.com/recipes/452625-missed-calls-on-android-sent-to-a-slack-channel

20. https://ifttt.com/recipes/300701-get-slack-notifications-about-assigned-trello-cards

21. http://ifttt.com/applets/8981p-keep-your-facebook-and-twitter-profile-pictures-in-sync

22. http://ifttt.com/applets/apKwXcPx-get-notified-when-your-favorite-artist-tweets-about-tickets-to-a-show

23. http://ifttt.com/applets/57744p-uber-receipts-to-evernote-for-expensify

24. http://ifttt.com/applets/176888p-get-a-daily-email-digest-with-ebay-listings-that-match-your-search

25. http://ifttt.com/applets/192151p-get-yourself-out-of-an-awkward-situation

(http://ifttt.com/applets/192151p-get-yourself-out-of-an-awkward-situation)

18. **Create an Evernote with a link to your location**[26] (http://ifttt.com/applets/255327p-create-a-note-with-a-link-to-your-location)

19. **Add to a Pinterest board when you include a specific #hashtag in your Insta caption**[27] (http://ifttt.com/applets/305886p-add-to-a-pinterest-board-when-you-include-a-specific-hashtag-in-your-insta-caption)

20. **Save Snapchat screenshots to Dropbox**[28] (http://ifttt.com/applets/102377p-save-snapchat-screenshots-to-dropbox)

21. **Wake up**[29] (https://ifttt.com/applets/Nrhz8uMQ-the-ultimate-wake-up-button)

22. **Goodnight** [30](https://ifttt.com/applets/UXqU3aTy-goodnight-all-tell-alexa-to-close-all-shades-turn-off-all-lights-and-lock-the-doors)

23. **Open Garage**[31] (https://ifttt.com/applets/374496p-open-the-garage-when-your-bmw-enters-the-driveway)

24. **Turn on lights** [32](**https://ifttt.com/applets/352044p-turn-on-your-hue-light-when-ring-detects-motion-at-your-door**)

25. **Washing** [33](https://ifttt.com/applets/398062p-get-a-

26. http://ifttt.com/applets/255327p-create-a-note-with-a-link-to-your-location

27. http://ifttt.com/applets/305886p-add-to-a-pinterest-board-when-you-include-a-specific-hashtag-in-your-insta-caption

28. http://ifttt.com/applets/102377p-save-snapchat-screenshots-to-dropbox

29. https://ifttt.com/applets/Nrhz8uMQ-the-ultimate-wake-up-button

30. https://ifttt.com/applets/UXqU3aTy-goodnight-all-tell-alexa-to-close-all-shades-turn-off-all-lights-and-lock-the-doors

31. https://ifttt.com/applets/374496p-open-the-garage-when-your-bmw-enters-the-driveway

32. https://ifttt.com/applets/352044p-turn-on-your-hue-light-when-ring-detects-motion-at-your-door

notification-when-your-samsung-washer-cycle-is-almost-done)

26. **Warm up your bed** [34](https://ifttt.com/applets/rcMFN4GR-turn-on-bed-warming-if-room-temperature-gets-too-cold)

27. **Close garage** [35](**https://ifttt.com/applets/253543p-check-and-close-the-garage-door-every-night-with-garageio**)

28. **Party with Google** [36](https://ifttt.com/applets/478777p-ok-google-party-time)

29. **Visual cues**[37] (https://ifttt.com/recipes/303614-when-amazon-echo-alexa-timer-hits-0-blink-hue-lights)

30. **Save water** [38] (https://ifttt.com/recipes/212029-save-water)

31. **Turn off Wi-Fi** [39](https://ifttt.com/recipes/302237-turn-off-wifi-when-you-leave-home-to-save-power)

32. **Get coffee** [40](https://ifttt.com/recipes/236859-fitbit-sleep-logging-turns-on-coffee-machine)

33. **Security** [41](**https://ifttt.com/recipes/187222-receive-a-video-recording-via-email-when-motion-is-detected**)

---

33. https://ifttt.com/applets/398062p-get-a-notification-when-your-samsung-washer-cycle-is-almost-done

34. https://ifttt.com/applets/rcMFN4GR-turn-on-bed-warming-if-room-temperature-gets-too-cold

35. https://ifttt.com/applets/253543p-check-and-close-the-garage-door-every-night-with-garageio

36. https://ifttt.com/applets/478777p-ok-google-party-time

37. https://ifttt.com/recipes/303614-when-amazon-echo-alexa-timer-hits-0-blink-hue-lights

38. https://ifttt.com/recipes/212029-save-water

39. https://ifttt.com/recipes/302237-turn-off-wifi-when-you-leave-home-to-save-power

40. https://ifttt.com/recipes/236859-fitbit-sleep-logging-turns-on-coffee-machine

41. https://ifttt.com/recipes/187222-receive-a-video-recording-via-email-when-motion-is-detected

34. **Match Lighting** [42](https://ifttt.com/recipes/93264-change-colors-of-lights-to-match-new-instagram-post)
35. **Get a text when house is hot** [43](https://ifttt.com/recipes/186774-temperature)
36. **Lights up** [44] **(https://ifttt.com/recipes/251790-dim-my-lights-to-a-golden-glow-when-the-sun-sets)**
37. **Liquor cabinet**[45] (https://ifttt.com/recipes/115640-call-me-if-the-liquor-cabinet-opens)
38. **Lock Door** [46](https://ifttt.com/recipes/265255-lock-your-door-when-leaving-home-network)
39. **Nest Correct** [47]**(https://ifttt.com/recipes/181568-if-the-temperature-outside-rises-above-___-then-set-your-nest-to-___)**
40. **Smoke alarm tweet** [48]**(https://ifttt.com/recipes/184879-if-your-nest-protect-detects-a-smoke-alarm-emergency-then-post-a-tweet)**

1. Tweet your Instagram as native photos on Twitter (http://ifttt.com/applets/103249p-tweet-your-instagrams-as-native-photos-on-twitter)

---

42. https://ifttt.com/recipes/93264-change-colors-of-lights-to-match-new-instagram-post

43. https://ifttt.com/recipes/186774-temperature

44. https://ifttt.com/recipes/251790-dim-my-lights-to-a-golden-glow-when-the-sun-sets

45. https://ifttt.com/recipes/115640-call-me-if-the-liquor-cabinet-opens

46. https://ifttt.com/recipes/265255-lock-your-door-when-leaving-home-network

47. https://ifttt.com/recipes/181568-if-the-temperature-outside-rises-above-___-then-set-your-nest-to-___

48. https://ifttt.com/recipes/184879-if-your-nest-protect-detects-a-smoke-alarm-emergency-then-post-a-tweet

CONCLUSION

This guide will show you how to get the very best from your new Alexa enabled devices within hours. With virtual assistant Alexa, Amazon has taken the entire Amazon experience to a completely new level. The Amazon Echo or Alexa enabled device can play your favorite music, movie, audiobook; answer about news, music, weather, traffic and more. This book will provide you with everything you need to know about the Alexa enabled devices.

OTHER BOOKS

———

BY *George Brown*

Kindle Device:

Everything You Need to Know about How to Delete Books, How to Add a Device to Amazon Account,

What is Kindle Unlimited and How it Works, How To Contact Amazon Kindle Customer Service

and More Useful Information about Your Kindle

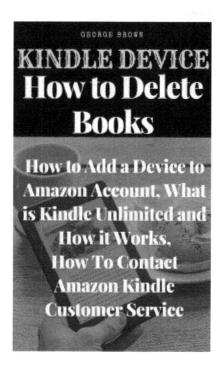

CHAPTER ELE KINDLE devices are one of the most popular and widely used devices. It is estimated that revenue from eBook sales in the U.S. in 2018 could reach 8.69 billion dollars from 2.31 billion in 2011. With so many users using various Kindle devices, a number of new model Kindle versions are released each year. The latest modes are: Kindle Fire 7", Kindle Fire HD, Kindle Fire 7" Kids edition, and Kindle Fire HD 8".

However, using the Kindle devices can cause some problems if you don't know how to use them properly. The book will provide you all the answers you seek and more.

Things you will learn from this book include:

Deleting books from your Kindle device with ease

Adding devices and registering Kindle devices

Everything you must know about Kindle Unlimited

Things you should know before buying your Kindle device

And Much, Much More!

Download your copy today!

New Kindle Fire Hd Owner's Manual

User Guide How to Unlock the Potential of Your Amazone Kindle Device

GEORGE BROWN

THE KINDLE FIRE HD is one of the most popular portable computing devices on the market right now. The device will help you perform computing tasks, read books, play games, listen to music, watch movies and thousands of other tasks once appropriate apps are installed.

If you just bought the new Kindle Fire HD tablet, and spend hours trying to figure out the device, then this book is the perfect book for you. This book is written to help the reader make full use of their Kindle Fire and get maximum benefit out of it. Inside this book, you will find step-by-step instructions with dozens of screenshots that walk you through the basic and advanced operations of your Kindle Fire HD.

With the help of the book go from a Kindle Fire beginner to expert in just 1 hour. You don't have to invest hours searching the web for answers; this complete Kindle Fire HD manual is the only thing you need. The guide is full of actionable steps, notes, hints, suggestions, and screenshots. This comprehensive user guide has it all – from simple step by step instructions for the beginner to tips and tricks for the more advanced user.

Learn all the hidden details about the Kindle Fire HD device you must have. With this book, you will learn 100% of what you need to know to get the most out of your new Fire tablet.

How this book helps you

How to properly set up and register your Kindle Fire

In an hour you can go from Kindle Fire beginner to Kindle Fire expert

Personalize your device

How to name your Kindle Fire

Buying with Kindle Fire HD

Uninstall apps

Manage notifications

Free up storage

Automatic backup

Filter out blue light

Browsing privately

Disable advertisement

Troubleshoot when problems arise

Download your copy today!

YOUR FREE GIFT

T*he free bonus will be waiting for you at this link*

https://mavro111.wixsite.com/istomin

Ethereum For Dummies

Everything You Need to Know About Ethereum, How to Mine Ethereum, How to Exchange Ethereum and How to Buy ETH

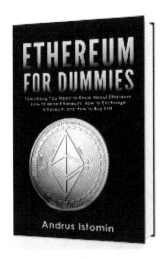

1

ETHEREUM AND BITCOIN are all the buzz right now. At the start of this year, the price of one Ethereum was only $10, but now it is currently trading aat $230. Experts predict the price of Ethereum will cross $1000 soon. More and more people are getting interested on Ethereum every day. The book provides you with all the necessary information you need to know and start investing on Ethereum. Written in simple language, the book is aimed at ordinary people who are eager to learn about Ethereum. This short, but compact book on Ethereum, will help anyone who is curious about Ethereum.

If you are among the millions who love to learn about investing, trade and new money making opportunities, then you have landed in the right place. Today, Ethereum is the fastest growingaltercoin. People are interested inEthereumnot only for its unique and advanced blockchain and smart contracts, but also as a potential digital asset. Currently, there are over 900 cryptocurrencies that exist, and it is extremely important to choose wisely and do your due diligence before investing your hard earned money on a specific digital currency. The book includes the best tips, tricks, and strategies that will lead to the highest profit possible with Ethereum.

In this book, you will learn

What is Ethereum?

Mining Ethereum

Mining Hardware and Software

Best Operating System for Mining

Ethereum Wallet

Tips, Tricks, and Strategies to Improving Mining Performance

How to Buy Ethereum

Things to Consider Before You Start Investing

And Much, Much More

The free bonus will be waiting for you at this link

https://mavro111.wixsite.com/istomin

Thanks for reading! Please add a short review and let me know what you thought!

Thanks and good luck!

George Brown

Don't miss out!

Visit the website below and you can sign up to receive emails whenever George Brown publishes a new book. There's no charge and no obligation.

https://books2read.com/r/B-A-HGHG-RSCT

BOOKS 2 READ

Connecting independent readers to independent writers.

Did you love *New Alexa Manual Tutorial to Unlock The True Potential of Your Alexa Devices. The Complete User Guide with Instructions*? Then you should read *Bitcoin Everything You Need to Know about Bitcoin, how to Mine Bitcoin, how to Buy BTC and how to Make Money with Bitcoin.* by Andru Istomin!

An alias Satoshi Nakamoto created Bitcoin, world's first cryptocurrency in 2008. The starting price of Bitcoin was around 2 cents per Bitcoin. In recent years, its growing popularity has caused its value to skyrocket. As of October 2017, the price of each Bitcoin is worth over $5000 and still rising. Over the last five years, Bitcoin investment outperformed popular investment sectors like real estate, gold, and stock. Experts are now saying that the price of 1 single Bitcoin could reach 10k within the next year. Currently, the Bitcoin is functioning as a people's currency, and there is a lot of hype surrounding Bitcoin.

Bitcoin has become a buzzword and has a far-reaching global impact. People who invested early on Bitcoin made a fortune, but it doesn't mean latecomers like you can't make a profit. If you are looking for a guide to know what Bitcoin is and how to invest and make a profit, then this Ultimate Bitcoin Guide is for you. This easy-to-read, easy-to-understand guide explains everything the reader needs to know about Bitcoin. This Bitcoin guidebook is for anyone who doesn't want to be left behind in the next technological revolution.

This book will explain everything that you need to know to get started with Bitcoin. In this book, you will find basic, accurate, detailed information that will help you understand what Bitcoin is. How you can use it to achieve your own needs, wants and goals. Apart from discussing the uses of Bitcoin in everyday life and business, the final chapter discusses a variety of ways you can make a profit with Bitcoin. This book is the asset that will change your views on the financial system, currency and investment. The clock is ticking, so don't take too long. Grab your copy today! Start to read the book and secure your financial fortune.

In this book you will learn:

IntroductionChapter 1 Bitcoin! What is it?Chapter 2 Bitcoin and BlockchainChapter 3 Bitcoin Address Chapter 4 Buying Your First BitcoinChapter 5 Using BitcoinChapter 6 Investing In BitcoinChapter 7 Doing Business with Bitcoin Chapter 8 Bitcoin Mining Chapter 9 Security Factor Chapter 10 Things You Should Know Chapter 11 Make Money with BitcoinConclusion Would You Like to Know More?

Scroll to the top and click that yellow button, and Get your copy Today!

Also by George Brown

New Alexa Manual Tutorial to Unlock The True Potential of Your Alexa Devices. The Complete User Guide with Instructions